The Kids' Guide to Government

How the Judicial Branch Works

Zelda Wagner

Lerner Publications ◆ Minneapolis

Lerner Publications Company
An imprint of Lerner Publishing Group, Inc.
241 First Avenue North
Minneapolis, MN 55401 USA

For reading levels and more information, look up this title
at www.lernerbooks.com.

Main body text set in Adrianna Regular.
Typeface provided by Chank.

Library of Congress Cataloging-in-Publication Data

Names: Wagner, Zelda, 2000– author.
Title: How the judicial branch works / Zelda Wagner.
Description: Minneapolis, MN : Lerner Publications , 2024. | Series: Searchlight books - the
    kids' guide to government | Includes bibliographical references and index. | Audience:
    Ages 8–11 | Audience: Grades 4–6 | Summary: "The judicial branch is an important
    part of the US government. It interprets laws and makes sure the constitution is
    being followed. Young readers learn about the judicial branch and how it impacts
    them"— Provided by publisher.
Identifiers: LCCN 2023039278 (print) | LCCN 2023039279 (ebook) | ISBN
    9798765626610 (library binding) | ISBN 9798765629628 (paperback) | ISBN
    9798765637166 (epub)
Subjects: LCSH: Courts—United States—Juvenile literature. | Justice, Administration of—
    United States—Juvenile literature.
Classification: LCC KF8720 .W34 2024 (print) | LCC KF8720 (ebook) | DDC 347/.73—
    dc23/eng/20230926

LC record available at https://lccn.loc.gov/2023039278
LC ebook record available at https://lccn.loc.gov/2023039279

Manufactured in the United States of America
1-1009929-51992-11/29/2023

Table of Contents

Chapter 1

INSIDE THE JUDICIAL BRANCH

In 2023, the Supreme Court ruled on a case about art. Years earlier, artist Andy Warhol made an image based on photographer Lynn Goldsmith's photo. He went on to make sixteen artworks with the photo.

Years later, a magazine used Warhol's image. Warhol had died so the magazine paid his foundation thousands of dollars. The magazine paid Goldsmith $400 for her photo. Goldsmith said she should get more money since her photo was used. Warhol's team said that he had changed the photo enough that it was a new work. The judicial branch takes over when people disagree about the laws. The two sides went to court to settle the argument.

Goldsmith (*right*) takes a photo with her lawyer outside of the Supreme Court building in 2022.

Inside the Courtroom

Judges are the most powerful members of the judicial branch. They are in charge of the court and decide if a person broke the law. During a trial like the one involving Warhol and Goldsmith, the judge listens carefully to the facts of a case. Sometimes a jury, a group of

people that give an opinion on a case, listens too.

The judge and jury decide who is right. Then the judge decides what will happen if the person broke a law. A judge agreed with Warhol's team and said that Goldsmith's photo had been changed enough to be a new work. But that wasn't the end of the case.

A Pyramid

The courts in the judicial branch are set up in different levels like a pyramid. If people disagree with a judge's decision, they can ask for another judge in a higher court to hear the case again. Goldsmith took her case to a higher court. This higher court disagreed with the lower court's decision and changed the ruling.

Deep Dive

The Supreme Court makes decisions for everyone in the United States. But for a long time, its justices did not look like a lot of the people in the country. A justice is a Supreme Court judge. Only white men served on the Supreme Court for almost two hundred years. Thurgood Marshall became the first Black justice in 1967. In 1981, Sandra Day O'Connor became the first woman on the court. In 2009, Sonia Sotomayor became the first Latina justice. Ketanji Brown Jackson became the first Black woman justice in 2022. The court has started to represent more of the people it serves.

The Supreme Court is the country's highest court. Nine judges, called justices, listen to cases from across the nation. They often choose cases where lower courts disagreed. They heard Warhol and Goldsmith's case after the two courts disagreed.

At least half the justices must agree for the Supreme Court to reach a decision. Seven of the justices decided that Goldsmith's photo wasn't changed enough to be a new work. She won the case.

The inside of the US Supreme Court building

Chapter 2

JUDICIAL BRANCH POWERS

The judicial branch is one of three branches, or parts, of the government. The others are the legislative and the executive branches. The legislative branch passes laws. The executive branch includes the president and the people who work for the president. This branch enforces laws. But the judicial branch has the power to decide what the laws mean.

The Court Systems

The US has federal courts and state courts. Most trials take place in state courts. Each state has its own set of lower and higher courts. They deal with people breaking state laws such as driving above the speed limit. If a person hurts another person, the trial usually takes place in a court in the state where the crime occurred.

ASSOCIATE JUSTICE LEONDRA KRUGER IS PART OF THE CALIFORNIA SUPREME COURT.

Federal courts hear cases that deal with people in more than one state and disagreements between states. Federal courts have another important job. They hear cases where federal laws, or laws for everyone in the nation, may have been broken. Federal courts can make decisions that affect everyone in the country.

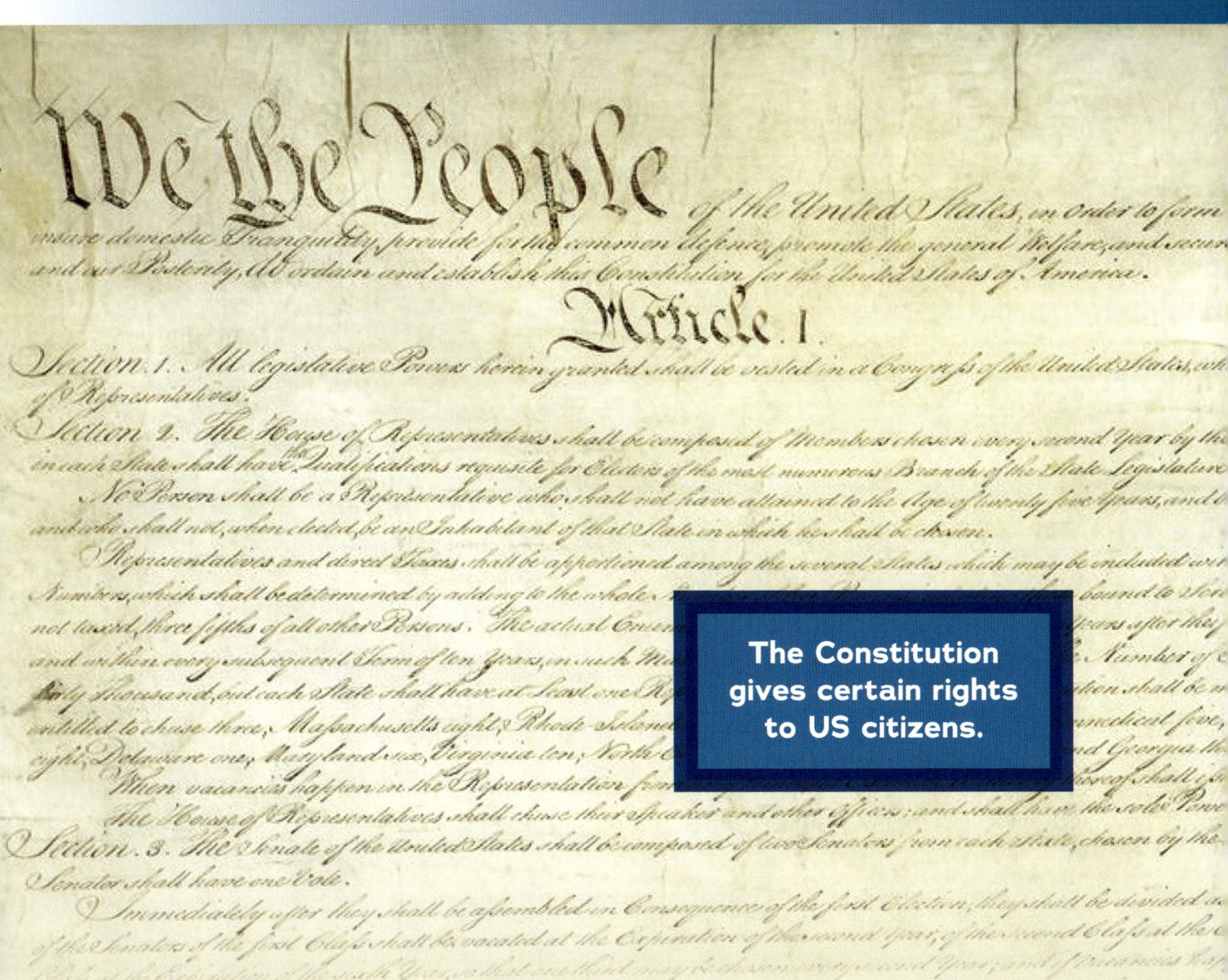

Protecting Freedoms

Federal judges use the rights listed in the US Constitution to guide their decisions. These rights appear in amendments to the Constitution. Amendments are changes to the Constitution. Federal courts hear cases where people believe that others have taken away their rights.

Making decisions is difficult for federal judges. They listen during trials to understand exactly what happened in each case. They review what other judges have decided in similar cases. They also have to think about what the Constitution's words mean. For example, the Constitution protects the freedom of people to express their opinions. Does that freedom include using someone's photo to make money? Judges have to decide.

A judge reads papers during a 2023 hearing.

Deep Dive

Social media lets people connect with one another. But sometimes it is used to send hurtful messages. Passing laws against this kind of behavior is hard because the Constitution protects the freedom of speech. But these online messages can be damaging. The Supreme Court decided that students cannot express opinions that take away the rights of other students. Laws give schools the power to make sure social media activity doesn't make another student feel unsafe at school.

Keeping Laws Fair

Courts do more than decide who is right in a case. Trials allow judges to see if laws are fair. Judges can ask for laws to be changed or removed if they decide a law takes away a person's constitutional rights.

For example, some old laws allowed states to separate students into different schools based on race. The Supreme Court decided that the government must treat all people equally. The court's decision meant that separating students took away people's rights under the Constitution.

JUSTICE FOR ALL

A judge's decisions can affect people's lives for years. Different court systems have different ways to decide who will be judges. In some states, voters elect judges. In other states, leaders of the state government might pick the judges. State judges serve for a set amount of time, or term. Most judges have terms from six to ten years.

Sharing Power

Federal judges are chosen differently from members of
the state courts. The Constitution gives the legislative
branch the power to decide the size and shape of the
federal court system. The executive branch also plays a
role in the federal court system. This is part of checks and
balances, a system of separating governmental powers.

People vote for Wisconsin's
Supreme Court justice in 2023.

The executive and legislative branches help choose federal judges and Supreme Court justices. The president announces a choice. Then a small group of members of the Senate votes to approve or reject the president's choice. After that, a larger group in the Senate votes. The president officially signs off on the new judge if the Senate approves.

Ketanji Brown Jackson speaks to the Senate before becoming a Supreme Court justice.

Neil Gorsuch becomes a
Supreme Court justice in 2017.

A Long Service

Federal judges can serve for the rest of their lives. Their decisions shape laws for much longer than the time that a president serves. Federal judges also keep their jobs longer than most members of the legislative branch are in office. Federal judges can be fired only if they break laws or do not do their jobs fairly.

Fair Treatment for All

The Constitution gives everyone rights. People accused of breaking a law have rights. These rights protect people at the time of an arrest and continue when they stand before a judge. For example, every person accused of a crime has the right to a speedy trial.

A lawyer speaks for her client, who was accused of a crime.

GET INVOLVED

Courts make decisions on everything from people's rights and freedoms to what information must be put on foods. Even if you never step foot in a courtroom, the court will still impact your life.

Classroom Courtrooms

Some schools have their own student governments that could include a judicial branch. Students there might decide if school rules are fair or if another student broke a rule. Your school might have a debate team. In debate, you can practice giving your case just as you might in a courtroom someday.

STUDENTS DEBATE DURING CLASS.

Adults can vote for the president and members of Congress, who will help choose federal judges. It's important to be active in government, including voting. You can learn about the people running for office even before you can vote. And you can encourage adults you know to vote.

Democracy and You

Have you and your friends ever had a disagreement? If disagreements arise, you can have a mock trial. The judge should be someone who hasn't made up their mind on the issue. The people who are disagreeing will each tell their side of the story. The judge will listen and ask questions. Then the judge will decide how to resolve the disagreement.

Know your Rights

You can always learn more about the judicial system even if you aren't able to vote or take part in a student judicial system. Know the rights you have in the US Constitution. Learn more about what the courts decided on different issues. These decisions could affect you.

Looking Ahead

For over two hundred years, judges in the judicial branch have decided how the Constitution protects the rights of people in the US. The document also says that rights listed in the Constitution are not the only ones people have. The judicial system continues to work to uphold the Constitution.

Supreme Court justices can stay in the court for life. Some people think Supreme Court justices should serve for limited terms. Some do not.

Some argue that lifetime service allows justices to make the best decisions. They do not need to worry about voters' opinions and can focus on the Constitution's rules.

But some feel that justices should have term limits so the court will have judges who will reflect the changing opinions of the American people.

Who is right? Should there be a term limit for justices? Why or why not?

Glossary

amendment: a change in the wording or meaning of the Constitution or another legal document

case: a set of facts or evidence to support one side of an argument

court: a place where legal cases are heard

executive: the branch of government that carries out laws and includes the president, vice president, and a presidential cabinet of advisers

federal: the national system

jury: local people who listen to a court case and decide who's innocent and who's guilty

legislative: the branch of government that makes laws and includes Congress

right: a privilege that cannot be taken away

ruling: a decision made by a court

term: a set amount of time for an elected official to hold office

Learn More

Ben's Guide: The Judicial Branch
    https://bensguide.gpo.gov/a-judicial

Britannica Kids: United States Supreme Court
    https://kids.britannica.com/kids/article/United-States-Supreme
    -Court/353827

Dolbear, Emily. *Ketanji Brown Jackson: Supreme Court Justice.* Parker, CO:
    Child's World, 2023.

National Geographic Kids: Three Branches of Government
    https://kids.nationalgeographic.com/history/article/three-branches
    -of-government

Vonder Brink, Tracy. *The Judicial Branch.* Coral Springs, FL: Seahorse,
    2022.

Wagner, Zelda. *How Checks and Balances Work.* Minneapolis: Lerner
    Publications, 2025.

Index

Photo Acknowledgments

Images: Mickey Osterreicher/Getty Images, p. 5; Gorodenkoff/Shutterstock, p. 6; Shutterstock, p.8; stock_photo_world/Shutterstock, p. 10; AP Photo/Jeff Chiu, p. 12; AP Photo/Mary Altaffer, p. 13; Library of Congress, p. 14; Alyssa Pointer-Pool/Getty Images, p. 15; FREDERIC J. BROWN/POOL/AFP via Getty Images, p. 17; AP Photo/Morry Gash, p. 19; Drew Angerer/Getty Images, p. 20; The Asahi Shimbun/Getty Images, p. 21; AP Photo/Octavio Jones/Pool Photo, p. 22; Marmaduke St. John/Alamy, p. 24; Sarah L. Voisin/The Washington Post/Getty Images, p. 25; Mayur Kakade/Getty Images, p. 27; Image by yeowatzup, courtesy of Wikimedia Commons (CC by 4.0 DEED), p. 28.

Cover: lusia83/Shutterstock; Shutterstock.